The Math of Focus, Creativity, and Deep Work

A Scientific and Practical Guide to Unlocking Your Brain's Full Potential

By Elara Juan Morris Mar 15, 2025

Thank you for picking up this book. I believe deeply in the potential of every reader to harness their mind's full capabilities. I invite you on this journey into the science and practice of deep, creative focus. Your feedback and stories inspire me; please feel free to reach out.

— Elara Juan Morris

Introduction

The Hidden Formula of Focus

The Modern Struggle for Attention

Imagine sitting at your desk, determined to tackle your most important task. You open your laptop, ready to work—but before you can even begin, a notification pops up, then another. You glance at your phone, intending to check it for just a second. Twenty minutes later, you're still scrolling.

By the time you refocus, your flow is gone; the spark of creativity has faded.

This struggle is not yours alone—it's shared by millions in today's attention economy. Social media platforms, email inboxes, and endless notifications have turned distraction into a daily habit, making deep, meaningful work feel nearly impossible.

Yet some people—writers, scientists, artists, entrepreneurs—produce extraordinary results in far less time than most of us spend merely "working."

What do they know that the rest of us don't?

They've mastered the math of focus, creativity, and deep work.

Why Some People Achieve More Than Others

We've long been told that success comes from working harder and longer. But history tells a different story.

- Albert Einstein developed the theory of relativity while working a full-time day job, harnessing short bursts of deep thinking to unlock groundbreaking ideas.

- Leonardo da Vinci spent years refining the Mona Lisa through structured, creative bursts rather than forcing inspiration.

- Nikola Tesla visualized entire electrical machines vividly in his mind before sketching anything, using extraordinary mental models and deep concentration.

These individuals weren't just naturally gifted. They structured their thinking in a way that made deep focus feel effortless.

What if you could do the same?

The Math of Focus, Creativity, and Deep Work

To illustrate why some achieve more, consider two workers: Person A and Person B.

- Person A works for eight hours a day but constantly checks email, scrolls social media, and jumps between tasks.

- Person B works for three hours a day in deep, uninterrupted sessions, free from distractions.

Who accomplishes more? Person B—every single time.

For decades, productivity advice has emphasized managing your time—implying success is about squeezing more hours into your day. But the truth is, productivity isn't about time; it's about attention.

Your effectiveness at work can be described by a simple but powerful formula:

$$Productivity \; = \; \frac{Time\ Spent \times Intensity\ of\ Focus}{Distractions + Cognitive\ Load}$$

When distractions increase, your focus intensity drops. When mental clutter (cognitive load) grows, productivity plummets. But when focus intensity increases, results improve exponentially.

Most people don't need more time; they need a system that works with their brain, not against it.

This book is about understanding this equation and applying it practically in your daily life.

The Impact of Focus Intensity on Work Output

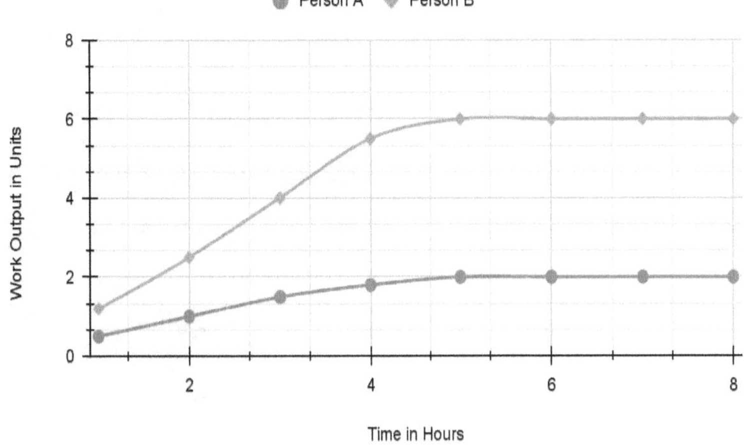

When distractions increase, your productivity drops
dramatically. Reducing distractions is the key to
exponential productivity gains.

How This Book Will Change the Way You Work

This book isn't merely about productivity hacks. It's about mastering the hidden equations that govern your ability to focus deeply, think creatively, and accomplish meaningful work.

Here's exactly what you'll learn:

- How to train your brain for deep, lasting focus.

- Why distractions feel addictive—and how you can break free.

- Techniques for entering a flow state consistently.

- Why managing your energy matters far more than managing your time.

- The hidden cognitive costs of multitasking—and how to avoid them.

- Practical ways to structure your day for maximum creativity and problem-solving.

By the end of this book, you'll have a proven system for achieving deep focus, eliminating distractions, and producing your best work yet.

Let's begin.

Chapter 1

The Law of Cognitive Load

Why Your Brain Struggles to Focus (and How to Fix It)

You sit down to work with the best intentions. Your to-do list is clear. Your laptop is open. Your coffee is hot.

Yet, within minutes, your attention begins to wander.

A Slack notification appears. An email distracts you. You suddenly remember something unrelated but important. Before you know it, you're juggling five different tasks, unable to deeply focus on any of them.

This isn't a lack of willpower—it's **cognitive overload**.

Your brain has a limited capacity to process information at any given time. When too many inputs compete for attention, your ability to focus collapses.

But what if you could optimize your cognitive load—reducing distractions, sharpening your focus, and unlocking deeper levels of thinking?

That's exactly what this chapter will teach you.

The Science Behind Cognitive Load

Your brain's working memory is like a small whiteboard—it can comfortably hold only about 4 to 7 pieces of information at a time before becoming overwhelmed.

Every additional task, notification, or distraction you introduce is like writing more items on the whiteboard. Eventually, space runs out, and your brain begins to erase previous information to accommodate new inputs.

This explains why you might read a long article and immediately forget half of it, or why frequent task-switching makes it challenging to remember important details.

The cognitive load equation:

$$Effective\ Focus = \frac{Working\ Memory\ Capacity - Distractions}{Task\ Complexity}$$

When distractions increase → focus decreases. When task complexity rises too high → your brain struggles.

The key to managing cognitive load—and improving productivity—is to optimize this equation by reducing distractions and simplifying complexity.

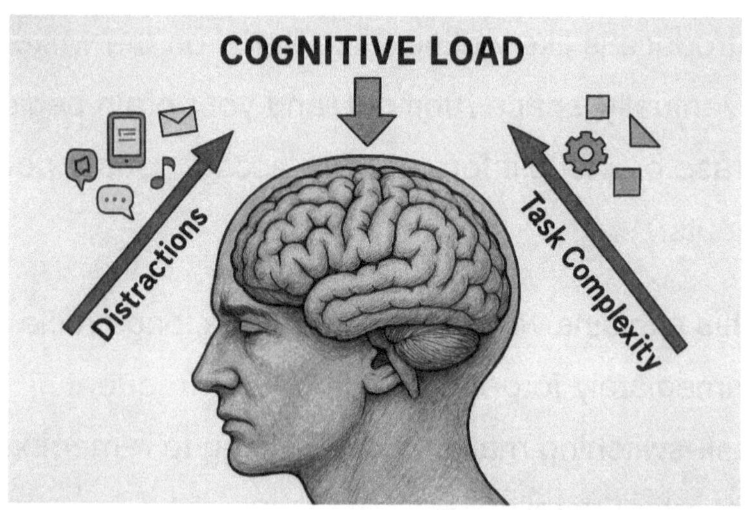

The Memory Test: Proof That Overload Kills Focus

Try this quick experiment:

Step 1: Read this number once:

7492038

Look away for 10 seconds, then recall it. Easy, right?

Step 2: Now try a longer number:

4920384710293847

Look away for 10 seconds and recall it. Difficult, isn't it?

This demonstrates the limits of your working memory. When your brain becomes overloaded, your ability to retain information and maintain deep focus deteriorates rapidly.

The Hidden Cost of Mental Overload

Cognitive overload doesn't merely reduce your focus—it actively diminishes your ability to think clearly. Overloaded brains experience:

- **Decision fatigue:** Choices become more challenging, leading to poorer judgment. When the brain is overwhelmed with information, its ability to make decisions deteriorates. This phenomenon, known as decision fatigue, results in choices becoming more challenging and judgment becoming poorer.Research indicates that individuals experiencing high cognitive load are more susceptible to making impulsive decisions and may struggle with self-regulation.

- **Mental exhaustion:** Even without physical exertion, your brain feels drained. Prolonged cognitive overload can lead to mental fatigue, where the brain feels drained despite the absence of physical exertion.

Studies have shown that mental fatigue impairs attention, memory, and decision-making abilities. For instance, research published in Frontiers in Psychology highlights that mental fatigue results in decreased performance in tasks requiring vigilance and sustained attention.

- **Increased stress:** Excess information generates anxiety, further diminishing productivity. An abundance of information can elevate stress levels, as the brain struggles to process excessive data. The Mayo Clinic Health System notes that cognitive overload can manifest as increased stress, fatigue, and frustration with daily activities.

If left unchecked, cognitive overload can escalate into burnout, procrastination, and a decline in work quality. Addressing and mitigating cognitive overload is crucial for maintaining optimal mental health and productivity.

How to Reduce Cognitive Load and Unlock Deep Focus

Improving focus requires reducing unnecessary cognitive strain. Here are three practical ways to achieve this immediately:

1. Clear Your Mental RAM

Just like a computer slows down with multiple open programs, your brain slows when juggling too many thoughts.

- **Write down pending thoughts:** Before starting deep work, spend five minutes listing everything on your mind. Offloading mental clutter frees valuable brainpower.

- **Adopt single-tasking:** Work deeply on one task at a time rather than constantly switching.

2. Optimize Your Work Environment

Your surroundings directly impact cognitive load.

- **Eliminate visual clutter:** A messy workspace increases mental clutter. Keep your area clean, minimal, and distraction-free.

- **Control auditory distractions:** If silence helps you concentrate, use noise-canceling headphones. Alternatively, employ ambient sounds like instrumental music or white noise.

3. Simplify Complex Tasks (Chunking Method)

Large projects often overwhelm, adding strain to your mental load. Break them down into smaller, manageable steps:

Instead of "write a report," break it into:

- Research the topic.

- Outline key points.

- Write the introduction.

Each smaller task is cognitively lighter, making deep work achievable without strain.

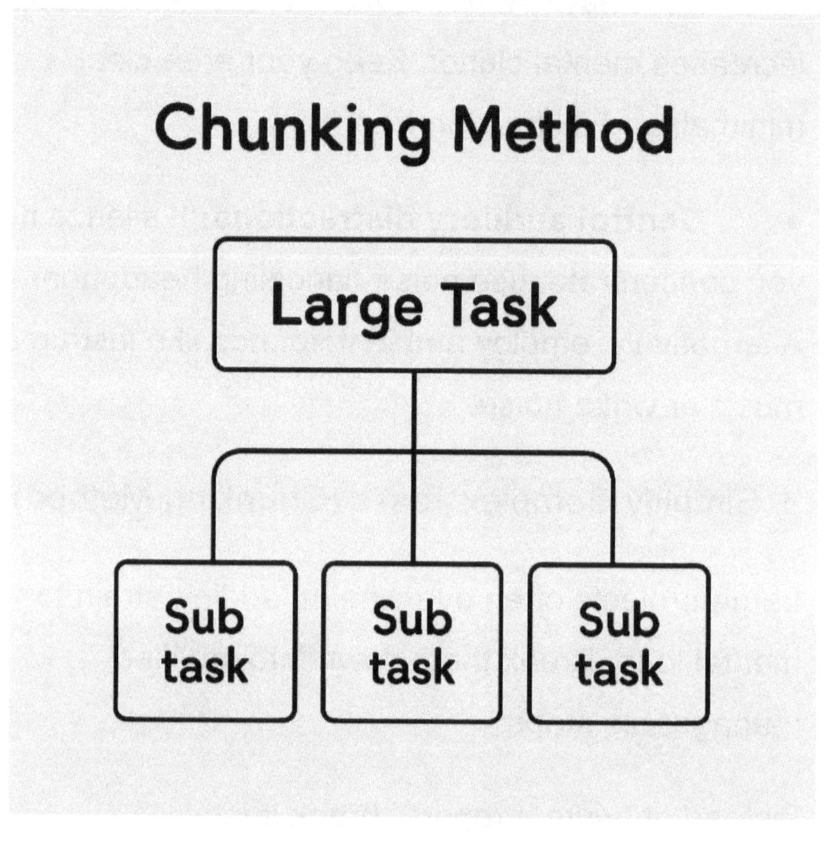

The Mental Clarity Equation: Your New Formula for Focus

By applying these principles, you can optimize cognitive load and train your brain for deeper concentration.

$$Mental\ Clarity = \frac{Task\ Simplicity + Distraction - Free\ Time}{Cognitive\ Load}$$

The more you reduce unnecessary inputs and simplify your tasks, the sharper your focus becomes.

The Power of an Uncluttered Mind

Before applying these strategies:

- Struggling to focus for longer than 10 minutes.

- Mental exhaustion early in the day.

- Multitasking without completing tasks effectively.

After applying these strategies:

- ★ Concentrating effortlessly for extended periods.

- ★ Completing tasks quicker with less mental effort.

- ★ Experiencing greater clarity and reduced stress.

Understanding The Law of Cognitive Load equips you to optimize your brain for deep, sustained focus.

Chapter Summary

Your brain's working memory is limited—protect it from overload.

Reduce distractions proactively by managing your environment and tasks carefully.

Single-tasking and chunking complex tasks improves your brain's efficiency dramatically.

Next Chapter: The Science of Deep Work

Now that you've learned to reduce cognitive load, the next step is mastering **Deep Work**—the state in which your brain achieves peak productivity.

In the following chapter, you'll discover:

- How to structure your day for deep focus.

- Why top performers protect deep work fiercely.

- Techniques for quickly transitioning into deep work.

Prepare yourself to unlock a new level of productivity and clarity.

References & Sources

- *Decision Fatigue – Wikipedia*
  _https://en.wikipedia.org/wiki/Decision_fatigue_

- *Mental Exhaustion: Effects of Cognitive Overload – Frontiers in Psychology (via Medium/PMC)*
  https://www.frontiersin.org/articles/10.3389/fpsyg.2019.00338/full

- *Cognitive Overload and Stress – Mayo Clinic Health System*
  https://www.mayoclinichealthsystem.org/hometown-health/speaking-of-health/mental-fatigue

Chapter 2

The Science of Deep Work

Why Some People Achieve More in Hours Than Others Do in Days

Picture two professionals working on the same project.

Michael spends ten hours at his desk, frequently checking emails, responding to messages, and constantly switching tasks. By day's end, he's exhausted, yet feels he's made minimal progress.

Sarah dedicates just four hours to deep, uninterrupted focus. By eliminating distractions, she completes her most important tasks before lunch—leaving the afternoon free for meetings, learning, and leisure.

They share the same job, but their results differ dramatically.

Why?

The difference isn't intelligence or motivation—it's the practice of **deep work**.

Deep work is the superpower of our distracted age, defined by intense concentration on a cognitively demanding task, completely free from distractions. Those who master it produce superior results in less time, while those stuck in shallow work fall behind.

This chapter explores the neuroscience behind deep work: why it's uniquely powerful, why many struggle to enter it, and practical strategies to train your brain for deep focus at will.

What is Deep Work? And Why Does It Matter?

Dr. Cal Newport, the author of *Deep Work*, defines it as:

"The ability to focus without distraction on a cognitively demanding task. It allows you to produce at an elite level, in less time, with greater quality."

Deep work matters because we live in a world designed to keep us distracted. Social media, endless notifications, and digital overload make it harder than ever to concentrate. Yet, those who can master deep work gain an unfair advantage in creativity, problem-solving, and career success.

$$Deep\ Work\ Output\ =\ \frac{Time\ Spent \times Focus\ Intensity}{Distractions + Mental\ Fatigue}$$

Deep work follows a simple principle:

When distractions increase → deep work suffers.
When mental fatigue rises → creativity declines.
But when focused attention increases → productivity
surges exponentially.

Now let's briefly explore the neuroscience behind why deep work is so transformative.

The Neuroscience of Deep Work

During deep work, your brain activates its prefrontal cortex—the area responsible for critical thinking, problem-solving, and intense concentration. Frequent task-switching, however, forces your brain into continual "context switching," burning mental energy and diminishing cognitive effectiveness.

Imagine your brain as a high-speed train: staying on a single track allows incredible acceleration. Constantly changing tracks, however, drastically slows its progress.

Deep work is simply the practice of staying on one cognitive track long enough to achieve peak productivity.

The Neuroscience of Deep Work

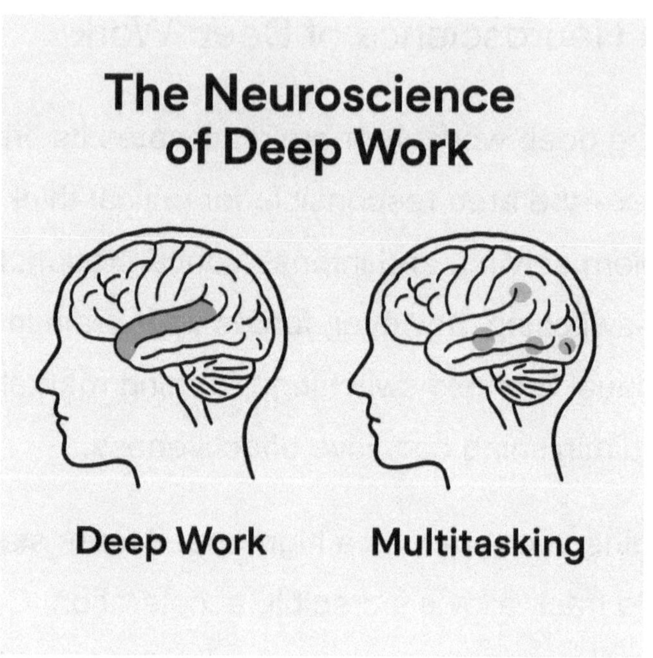

Research indicates that the prefrontal cortex plays a crucial role in task-switching and cognitive flexibility. Studies have shown that task-switching involves increased activation in the prefrontal cortex, and that damage to this area can impair the ability to switch tasks effectively. Additionally, task-switching is associated with reaction time costs, as the brain requires time to adjust to new tasks.

The Hidden Cost of Distraction

Consider two more professionals—Lisa and Mark.

Lisa begins her day by scheduling three uninterrupted hours of deep work. She eliminates distractions, sets a clear goal, and completes a campaign strategy capable of generating significant revenue.

Mark spends the same three hours reacting to Slack, emails, and minor tasks. He feels busy yet produces minimal valuable work.

Over time, Lisa strengthens her capacity for complex thought, while Mark's brain becomes conditioned to distraction. Their results diverge not due to talent, but rather how they manage their attention.

How Your Brain Enters Deep Focus

Deep work requires understanding your brain's two operational modes clearly:

1. Focused Mode (Deep Work):

- Engages the prefrontal cortex.

- Ideal for complex, challenging tasks.

- Enhances creativity, insight, memory, and rapid problem-solving.

2. Diffused Mode (Shallow Work):

- Activated by multitasking and task-switching.

- Leads to superficial thinking, reduced creativity, and slower progress.

Deep focus is the intentional shift into Focused Mode. Task-switching prevents your brain from reaching this peak cognitive state, leaving you stuck in shallow, inefficient patterns.

Brain scans show that people in deep work states experience increased activity in the prefrontal cortex, leading to:

- Higher creativity and insight

- Stronger memory retention

- Faster learning and problem-solving

The True Cost of Shallow Work

Most workers constantly jump between emails, notifications, and messages, believing themselves productive. But research reveals the true impact of frequent interruptions:

Cognitive Switching Penalty = Time Lost + Mental Fatigue + Increased Errors

- It takes an average of 23 minutes to regain deep focus after a distraction.

- Constant context switching reduces productivity by up to 40%.

- Multitasking increases mistakes and reduces information retention.

Simply checking your phone five times daily can waste nearly two hours—every day.

Successful people don't work longer—they deliberately eliminate shallow work.

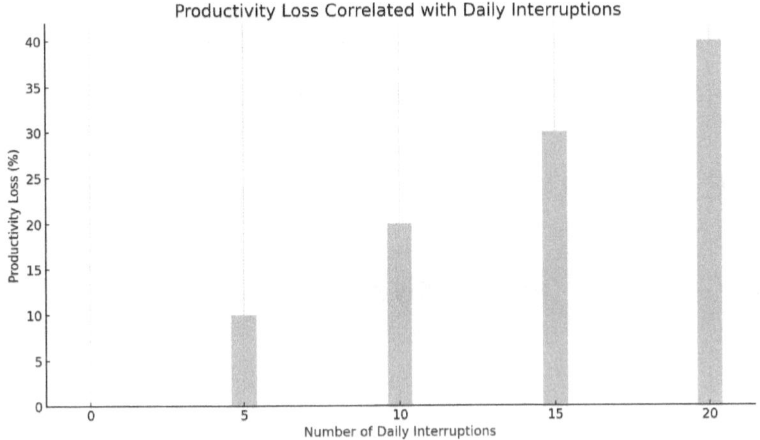

How to Train Your Brain for Deep Work

Like strength training or mastering an instrument, deep work is a skill that improves with practice. Here's a clear, step-by-step approach to training your brain:

1. Create a Distraction-Free Work Zone:

- Work consistently in one dedicated space.

- Remove all digital and environmental distractions.

- Use noise control methods (headphones, instrumental music).

2. Set a Clear Deep Work Schedule:

- Prioritize deep work first thing each morning, before your attention can be hijacked.

- Use 90-minute deep work blocks followed by intentional 15-minute breaks.

- Define clear stopping points to prevent cognitive fatigue.

3. Apply the 20-Minute Rule to Enter Deep Focus Faster:

Your brain requires approximately 20 uninterrupted minutes to transition fully into deep focus. Accelerate this transition by:

- Completing a brief, consistent ritual (stretching, breathing exercises, journaling).

- Setting a timer and committing fully to a distraction-free environment.

After crossing the 20-minute threshold, sustaining deep work becomes significantly easier.

From Shallow to Deep Work

Before mastering deep work:

- Difficulty concentrating beyond 15 minutes.

- Constant distraction and mental fatigue.

- Busy but not productive.

After mastering deep work:

- ★ Effortless concentration for hours.

- ★ Higher-quality work produced in less time.

- ★ Greater control of your mental energy and time.

Chapter Summary

Deep work dramatically outperforms shallow multitasking.

Protecting your attention unlocks creativity and productivity.

Regular practice of deep work trains your brain for sustained, elite performance

Having understood the neuroscience of deep work and its profound benefits, you're now ready to explore the hidden psychological factors behind your brain's craving for distraction.

Next Chapter: The Hidden Enemies of Focus

Having learned how to effectively structure your day for deep work, it's now crucial to address distractions at their source. In Chapter 3, you'll uncover why your brain is naturally drawn to interruptions and how to rewire these impulses toward lasting focus.

References & Sources

- *It takes an average of 23 minutes to regain deep focus after a distraction*
Gloria Mark, UC Irvine study -
https://www.themuse.com/advice/this-is-nuts-it-takes-nearly-30-minutes-to-refocus-after-you-get-distracted

- *Constant task-switching reduces productivity by up to 40%*
Dr. David Meyer, University of Michigan – Published by the American Psychological Association -
https://www.apa.org/topics/research/multitasking

- *Multitasking significantly increases errors and reduces information retention*
Stanford University research on media multitasking -
https://news.stanford.edu/stories/2018/10/decade-data-reveals-heavy-multitaskers-reduced-memory-psychologist-says

- *"Functional Neuroanatomy of the Human Prefrontal Cortex" – A comprehensive overview of the prefrontal cortex and its role in high-level cognition: https://www.ncbi.nlm.nih.gov/pmc/articles/PMC3182007*

- *"The Neuroscience of Focus and Attention" – Discusses how the brain sustains attention and the regions involved, especially the prefrontal cortex: https://www.sciencedirect.com/science/article/pii/S13646661319302446*

- *"Cognitive Control in Task Switching" – From Frontiers in Human Neuroscience, explains the energy and brain region demands of switching tasks: https://www.frontiersin.org/articles/10.3389/neuro.09.002.2007/full*

- *"Cognitive Switching and Mental Fatigue" – A study showing measurable delays and reduced accuracy when the brain shifts between tasks:*

Chapter 3

The Hidden Enemies of Focus

Why Your Brain Loves Distractions (and How to Break Free)

You sit down to tackle an important task, determined to maintain your focus.

Moments later, without realizing it, you reach for your phone. You scroll through social media. An email demands your attention. A notification buzzes.

Every time you check your phone or respond to an alert, your brain releases dopamine—the chemical that rewards you for seeking new information. This creates a powerful habit loop:

Trigger (Notification) → Action (Check Phone) → Reward (Dopamine Boost)

Before you know it, thirty minutes vanish, and your original task is forgotten. Despite promising yourself, "it won't happen again," this pattern repeats itself, day after day.

Why?

Your brain is wired to seek distractions.

Most people don't lose focus due to a lack of discipline—they lose it because they haven't addressed the hidden triggers hijacking their attention. In this chapter, you'll learn to identify these hidden enemies of deep work and acquire tools to break free from distraction.

DOPAMINE

The Cost of Constant Context Switching

Imagine you're writing an important report or coding a complex program. Just as you reach deep concentration, an email notification appears. You think, "I'll quickly check it."

Five minutes later, you return to your original task—but your brain continues processing the distraction in the background, creating a costly interruption.

Total Time Lost = Task Switching Penalty + Refocus Delay

- It takes approximately **23 minutes** to regain deep focus after one distraction.

- Five interruptions daily can cost nearly two hours of productivity each day.

- Over a year, that equates to over a month of wasted work time.

Each interruption trains your brain for shallow thinking, making it progressively more difficult to achieve deep work.

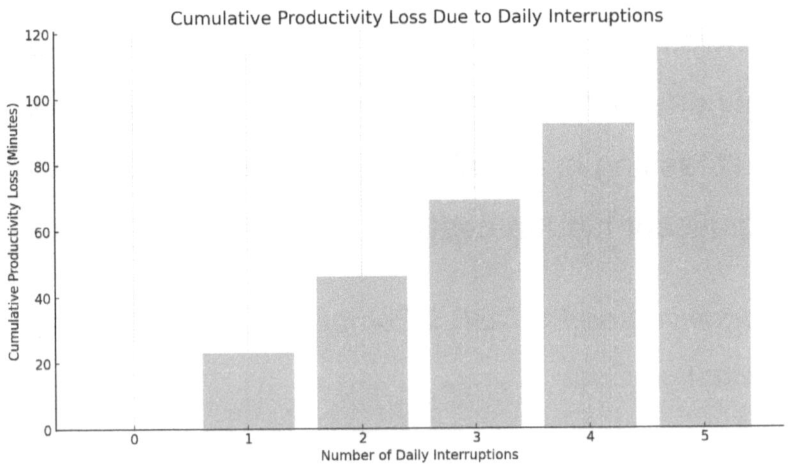

The Multitasking Myth: Why Your Brain Can't Handle It

Many pride themselves on multitasking. Yet research consistently shows your brain can effectively handle only one complex task at a time. What feels like multitasking is actually rapid task-switching, incurring significant hidden costs:

Cognitive Load = Task 1 Complexity + Task 2 Complexity + Switching Cost

- **Slower Processing Speed** – Every time you switch tasks, your brain has to **reset and refocus**, slowing you down.

- **More Mistakes** – Studies show that multitaskers **make more errors** because their attention is split.

- **Increased Mental Fatigue** – Constant switching drains your brain's energy, leaving you **exhausted.**

To accomplish more meaningful work, the solution isn't to multitask faster, but rather to eliminate multitasking entirely.

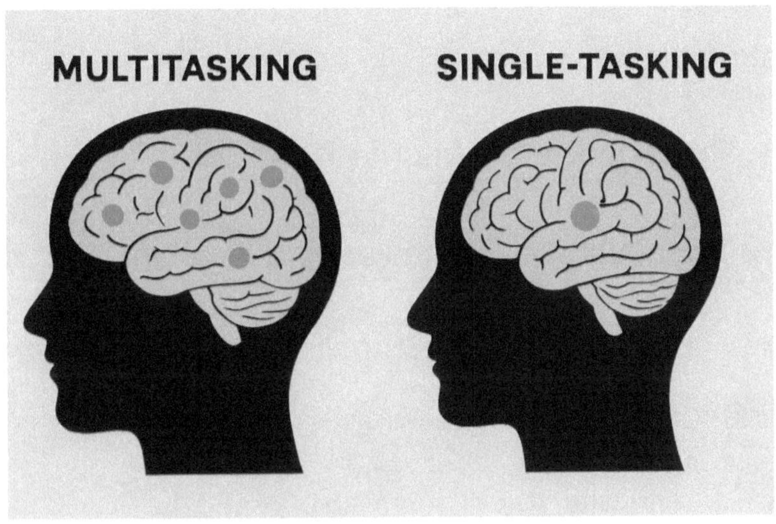

Breaking Free from the Dopamine Distraction Loop

To regain control of your attention, use these proven strategies:

1. Practice the 10-Minute Rule

Your brain craves immediate gratification. To retrain it:

- When you feel compelled to check your phone, pause for 10 minutes.

- Usually, the craving fades quickly.

- Over time, this technique weakens your brain's addiction to interruptions.

2. Batch Shallow Work

Avoid random email checks and scattered admin tasks throughout your day. Instead:

- Check emails and messages at set times—ideally, once in the morning and once in the afternoon.

- Schedule less cognitively demanding tasks during low-focus periods (e.g., after lunch or late afternoon).

This preserves your highest-energy periods exclusively for deep work.

3. Establish a Deep-Focus Ritual

Create a simple routine that signals to your brain: it's time to focus deeply.

- Close all non-essential tabs and apps.

- Put your phone on airplane mode or keep it physically distant.

- Clearly define your task objective for the work session.

Over time, this routine conditions your mind to enter deep focus swiftly and effortlessly.

The Focus Mastery Equation: Designing a Life That Supports Deep Work

$$Sustained\ Focus\ =\ \frac{Distraction - Free\ Environment + Cognitive\ Clarity}{Interruptions + Task\ Switching}$$

Reducing interruptions, maintaining cognitive clarity, and protecting your deep work sessions allows your brain to achieve consistently higher productivity levels. Ultimately, you'll accomplish more meaningful work in four focused hours than most people achieve in a scattered eight-hour workday.

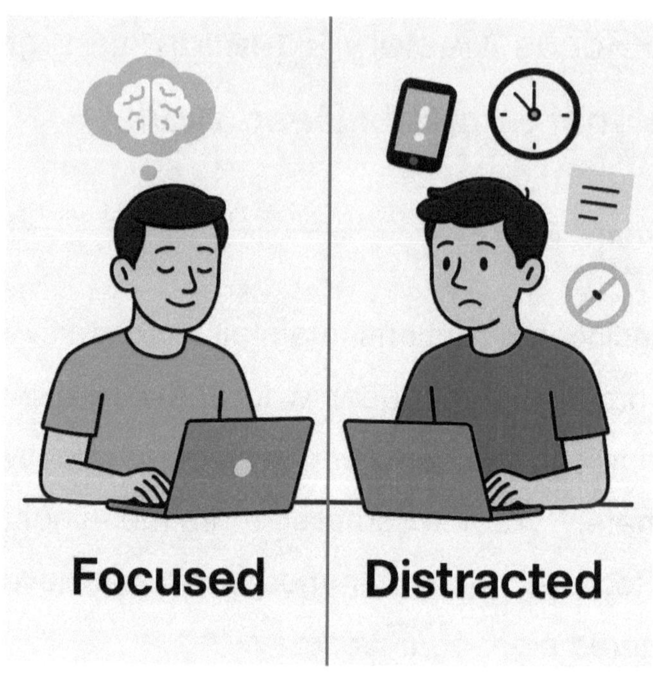

Focused
Distracted

The Power of Eliminating Hidden Focus Killers

Before addressing hidden distractions:

- Frequent impulsive phone-checking

- Difficulty sustaining attention beyond 15 minutes

- Feeling exhausted without meaningful progress

After addressing hidden distractions:

- ★ Consistent entry into deep work

- ★ Higher-value output in shorter time frames

- ★ Increased sense of control over your attention and time

Chapter Summary

Your brain seeks distractions due to dopamine-driven reward loops.

Frequent interruptions cause significant productivity loss and mental fatigue.

Strategic interventions—like batching shallow tasks and establishing focus rituals—break the distraction cycle, enabling deeper, more productive work.

Next Chapter: The 4-Hour Deep Work System

Having identified and addressed the hidden enemies of deep work, you're now ready to implement a structured approach for consistent productivity. In Chapter 4: The 4-Hour Deep Work System, you'll learn exactly how to structure your day around focused productivity, shallow task management, and cognitive recovery.

References & Sources

1. *Why Distractions at Work Take Longer to Recover From Than You Think (UC Irvine Study) -* *https://www.themuse.com/advice/this-is-nuts-it-takes-nearly-30-minutes-to-refocus-after-you-get-distracted*

2. *Multitasking: Switching Costs – American Psychological Association -* *https://www.apa.org/topics/research/multitasking*

3. *How Multitasking Harms Your Brain and Productivity – Cleveland Clinic -* *https://health.clevelandclinic.org/multitasking-harms-productivity*

4. *Dopamine, Smartphones & You: A Battle for Your Time – Harvard University -* *https://sitn.hms.harvard.edu/flash/2018/dopamine-smartphones-battle-time*

Chapter 4

The 4-Hour Deep Work System

Why Working More Hours Doesn't Equal More Productivity

It's 9:00 AM, and Daniel is at his desk, determined to have a productive day. His calendar overflows with back-to-back meetings, urgent emails flood his inbox, and a lengthy to-do list awaits him.

He works hard—sometimes late into the night—yet at day's end, he still feels he accomplished little meaningful work.

Sound familiar?

Most people assume productivity means working more hours. In truth, productivity hinges on the intensity and quality of your attention, not how long you sit at your desk.

Historically, great achievers—authors, scientists, and entrepreneurs—have consistently prioritized brief, highly-focused work sessions rather than prolonged hours of distracted labor.

This is precisely where the **4-Hour Deep Work System** excels.

Why 4 Hours of Deep Work Beats 10 Hours of Shallow Work

Most professionals spend their days reacting—answering emails, attending meetings, and completing low-impact tasks. Consider the difference between two professionals:

- James: Works ten hours daily, mostly in meetings, emails, and routine tasks. He's mentally exhausted but makes little progress on important projects.

- Sarah: Works just four hours daily in deep, uninterrupted focus on essential projects, free from distractions. She consistently produces superior results.

Who accomplishes more? Sarah—every time.

$$Productivity = \frac{Deep\ Work\ Hours \times Focus\ Intensity}{Distractions + Task - Switching\ Penalty}$$

The key to **elite-level productivity** isn't working longer—it's **structuring your day around deep work.**

The 4-Hour Deep Work Formula: A Proven Structure

This structured approach will maximize your daily productivity:

Hour 1: Start with Deep Work

Instead of immediately responding to emails or messages, reserve the first 90 minutes for uninterrupted, high-value tasks.

- Identify your most critical task each morning.

- Eliminate all distractions—emails, phone, notifications.

Hour 2: Second Deep Work Block

After a short 10–15 minute break, engage in another 90-minute deep work session.

- Reserve this block for challenging, cognitively-demanding tasks.

- Avoid interruptions to sustain high productivity.

By lunchtime, your essential tasks are complete, leaving your afternoon flexible and less stressful.

Afternoon: Shallow Tasks & Recovery

Mental energy naturally dips in the afternoon—perfect for lower-intensity tasks:

- Emails, administrative tasks, routine calls.

- Meetings requiring less intense cognitive effort.

Attempting deep work when fatigued usually results in reduced quality and productivity.

Evening: Recharge and Prepare

Many continue working late, mistaking busyness for productivity. However, optimal performance requires intentional rest:

•	End your workday at least two hours before bedtime.

•	Engage in restorative activities (e.g., reading, gentle exercise).

•	Briefly plan tomorrow's deep work sessions to prime your brain.

The Science Behind the 4-Hour Deep Work System

esearch reveals our brains function optimally in **90-minute ultradian cycles**, designed for bursts of intense focus followed by short recovery periods.

- Short, intense work sprints are significantly more productive than prolonged, distracted effort.

- The brain's prefrontal cortex operates at peak performance during these focused intervals.

- Cognitive fatigue typically sets in after 4–5 hours of intense concentration, diminishing returns thereafter.

Aligning your work schedule with these natural cycles results in consistently high productivity.

$$Optimal\ Focus\ Time = 90\ min\ deep\ work + 15\ min\ break$$

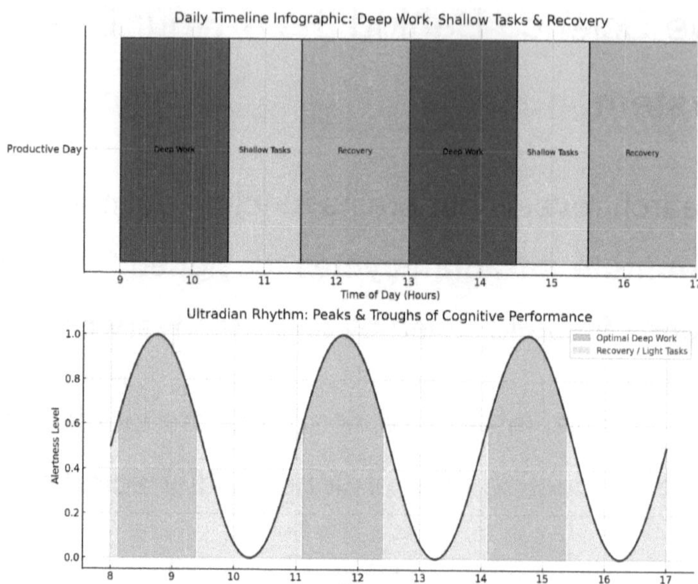

Daily Timeline Infographic: Deep Work, Shallow Tasks & Recovery
Productive Day
Deep Work
Shallow Tasks
Recovery
Deep Work
Shallow Tasks
Recovery
Time of Day (Hours)
Ultradian Rhythm: Peaks & Troughs of Cognitive Performance
Optimal Deep Work
Recovery / Light Tasks
Alertness Level
Time of Day (Hours)

Transforming Your Productivity

Before applying the 4-Hour Deep Work System:

●   Long hours spent working with minimal impactful outcomes.

●   Frequent mental exhaustion and burnout.

●   Difficulty carving out time for truly meaningful tasks.

After applying the system:

★   Major tasks completed before midday.

★   Enhanced control of your time and attention.

★   Higher-quality results achieved in significantly less time.

Chapter Summary

Productivity is about deep, intentional work—not extended work hours.

Structuring your day around two focused 90-minute sessions yields optimal productivity.

Scheduling shallow work later in the day aligns better with your natural cognitive energy levels.

Rest and recovery periods are essential to maintaining sustained high productivity.

Next Chapter: Mastering Energy for Maximum Focus

Now that you've mastered structuring your day for optimal productivity, the next step is ensuring sustained mental energy. In **Chapter 5: Mastering Energy for Maximum Focus**, you'll learn how to manage your cognitive resources effectively—enabling consistent, effortless focus throughout your entire day.

References & Sources

1.   *"A 90-Minute Plan for Personal Effectiveness" – Harvard Business Review - https://hbr.org/2011/01/the-most-important-practice-ihbr.org*

2.   *"The Workplace Is Killing People and Nobody Cares" – Stanford Graduate School of Business - https://www.gsb.stanford.edu/insights/workplace-killing-people-nobody-caresStanford Graduate School of Business+2Stanford Graduate School of Business+2Stanford Graduate School of Business+2*

3.   *"After Two Years Of Trying 6-Hour Workdays, These Companies Say It Worked" – Fast Company - https://www.fastcompany.com/3067325/after-two-years-of-trying-6-hour-workdays-these-companies-say-it-worked*

Chapter 5

Mastering Energy for Maximum Focus

Why Your Focus Depends More on Energy Than on Time

At 3:00 PM, David sits at his desk, staring blankly at the screen. His to-do list remains long, but his brain simply refuses to cooperate. He isn't out of time—he's out of energy.

Like most people, David assumed productivity was a matter of time management. But sustained concentration isn't primarily about how many hours you work—it's about effectively managing your mental energy.

Even with extra hours in your day, low cognitive energy renders those hours ineffective. High performers understand this and prioritize energy management to maintain consistent productivity.

In this chapter, you'll learn:

- The neuroscience behind mental energy and focus.

- How to identify your natural energy peaks and valleys.

- Practical methods to optimize your mental energy throughout the day.

Understanding Mental Energy: Your Brain's Fuel System

Your brain is energy-intensive, consuming roughly 20% of your body's daily energy supply. Mental energy typically follows a predictable daily pattern:

- **Morning:** Highest cognitive energy; optimal for deep focus.

- **Afternoon:** Energy dips, increasing vulnerability to distractions.

- **Evening:** Energy further declines; ideal time for restorative activities.

Understanding and aligning tasks with your body's natural rhythms is key to sustained productivity.

Your brain's energy levels directly dictate your capacity for sustained focus:

Your brain doesn't have unlimited energy—if you don't protect and optimize it, your ability to focus will suffer.

$$Sustained\ Focus\ =\ \frac{Energy\ Levels \times Cognitive\ Efficiency}{Decision\ Fatigue + Mental\ Exhaustion}$$

When energy is high, focus is strong.
When energy drops, focus collapses.

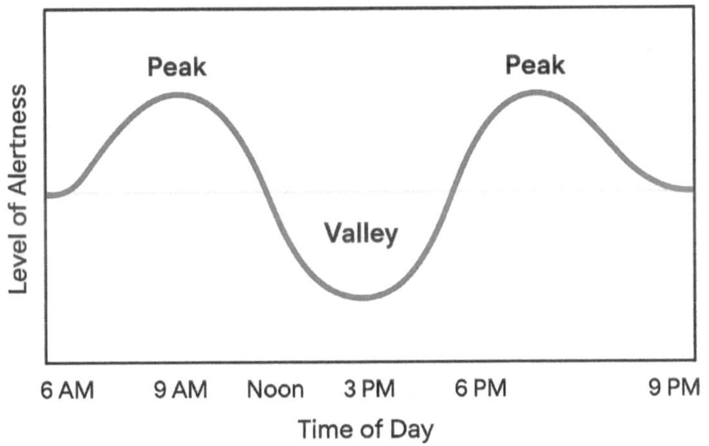

Daily Cognitive Energy

Managing mental energy—rather than simply managing time—is critical to achieving lasting productivity.

The Energy Optimization Formula: How to Stay Sharp All Day

To get the most out of your brainpower, you must align your work with your body's natural energy rhythms.

Consistent Focus = Aligning Tasks with Energy Peaks + Avoiding Mental Drains + Strategic Recovery

Below are three practical strategies to maintain peak energy and focus throughout your day.

1. Work With Your Natural Energy Peaks

Your brain performs best during predictable energy peaks:

- **Morning (8 AM–12 PM):** Reserve this time for deep, complex tasks requiring maximum cognitive effort.

- **Afternoon (1 PM–4 PM):** Ideal for routine tasks, administrative duties, and meetings.

- **Evening (6 PM onward):** Prioritize rest and recovery to recharge mental energy.

2. Avoid Major Energy Drains

Protect your cognitive resources by minimizing these common energy drains:

- **Decision Fatigue:** Excessive decision-making rapidly exhausts mental resources.

  - Automate routine decisions (meals, clothing, morning routine).

  - Plan your tasks the evening before.

- **Task Switching:** Rapidly switching between tasks severely taxes cognitive energy.

  - Batch similar tasks together.

  - Schedule fixed times for emails and communications.

- **Information Overload:** Excessive consumption of digital content clutters mental clarity.

  - Limit content consumption to relevant, high-quality information.

  - Replace passive consumption with intentional creation or reflection.

3. Recharge Strategically Throughout the Day

Your brain requires brief recovery periods to sustain performance:

- **Micro Break (5–10 mins):** Short walk or deep-breathing exercises refresh cognitive function.

- **Mid-Level Break (20–30 mins):** Moderate activity like walking, stretching, or a brief power nap.

- **Evening Recovery:** Intentional rest, engaging hobbies, and quality sleep to fully recharge cognitive reserves.

Avoid "fake breaks," like scrolling social media, which further deplete mental resources.

Transforming Your Daily Energy Management

Before optimizing energy:

- Difficulty focusing in afternoons.

- Persistent feelings of mental exhaustion.

- Working many hours with limited productivity.

After energy optimization:

★ Sustained high-level focus throughout the day.

★ Improved productivity with less effort.

★ Clearer thinking, reduced stress, and greater satisfaction.

Chapter Summary

Productivity depends primarily on managing cognitive energy—not just time.

Align your tasks with your brain's natural energy peaks and valleys.

Minimize energy drains like decision fatigue, multitasking, and information overload.

Schedule strategic recovery breaks to sustain cognitive performance throughout the day.

Next Chapter: The Flow Code—Unlocking Effortless Focus

Having optimized your daily energy management, you're now equipped to consistently reach deeper levels of focus. Next, you'll discover how to enter the ultimate state of effortless productivity: **Flow**. In **Chapter 6: The Flow Code**, you'll learn practical strategies for consistently accessing this peak cognitive state.

References & Sources

1.	*Decision Fatigue Exhausts Cognitive Resources – American Psychological Association -* *https://www.apa.org/news/press/releases/2011/03/decision-fatigue*

2.	*Ultradian Rhythms: Leveraging Natural Energy Cycles for Productivity – Harvard Business Review -* *https://hbr.org/2011/01/the-most-important-practice-i*

3.	*Information Overload and its Impact on Productivity – Deloitte Insights -* *https://www2.deloitte.com/us/en/insights/focus/technology-and-the-future-of-work/using-technology-to-reduce-information-overload.html*

Chapter 6

The Flow Code - Unlocking Effortless Focus

How to Consistently Enter the Peak State of Productivity

Have you ever been so absorbed in a task that time seemed to disappear? Athletes call this "being in the zone." Writers and artists know it as a creative flow. Psychologists describe it as a state of optimal cognitive performance.

Regardless of what you call it, **Flow** is a state of effortless focus, where ideas and productivity surge naturally, free of resistance.

Imagine entering this state on demand. That's exactly what this chapter will teach you: how to consistently access the powerful cognitive state known as Flow.

Understanding Flow: Peak Productivity and Effortless Focus

Renowned psychologist Mihaly Csikszentmihalyi defines Flow as:

"A state of complete immersion in an activity where your skills perfectly match the challenge, resulting in deep enjoyment, effortless focus, and peak performance."

Research indicates individuals in Flow states experience productivity boosts of up to 500%.

Throughout history, groundbreaking achievements have emerged from Flow: Newton's laws of motion, Beethoven's symphonies, Einstein's theory of relativity. These breakthroughs didn't happen by accident—they arose during sustained periods of deep, uninterrupted focus.

The Flow Formula: Balancing Skill and Challenge

To enter a state of deep, effortless focus, you must balance three key elements:

$$Flow = (Challenge\ Level \times SKill\ Level) - Distractions$$

Here's how it works:

1. Challenge Level: The task must be difficult enough to keep you engaged but not so hard that it overwhelms you.

2. Skill Level: You need to have enough experience or knowledge to handle the challenge. If it's too easy, you'll get bored. If it's too hard, you'll get frustrated.

3. Distractions: If your focus is constantly broken, you'll never enter flow—your mind needs complete immersion to get into this state.

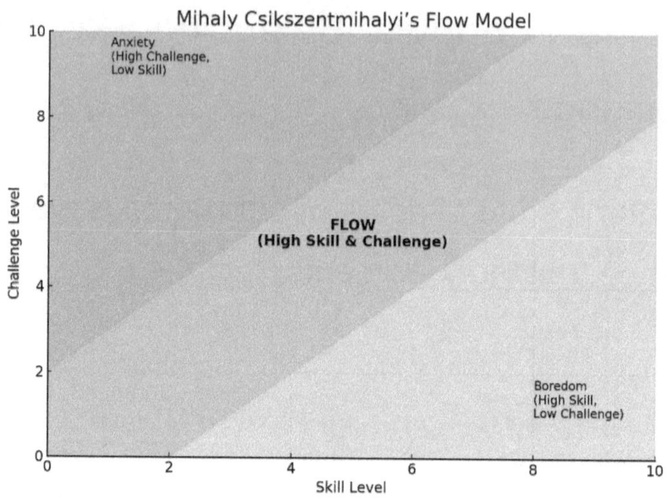

When challenge and skill are balanced—neither too easy nor overwhelming—and distractions are minimized, Flow emerges naturally.

How to Trigger Flow Consistently

You don't have to wait for Flow to happen spontaneously. You can deliberately create the conditions necessary to enter this state:

1. Set Clear, Specific Goals

Vague goals prevent deep immersion. Clearly defined objectives focus your attention fully.

Instead of:

- "Work on project"

Try:

- "Write 1,000 words of my report."

- "Complete three design concepts."

- "Solve this coding challenge."

Clear goals direct your attention, making it easier to slip into Flow.

2. Eliminate Distractions

Flow requires uninterrupted concentration. Eliminate distractions proactively:

- Turn off notifications.

- Silence or store your phone elsewhere.

- Inform others that you'll be unavailable during deep-work sessions.

3. Use the 90-Minute Deep Work Sprint

Research shows your brain enters Flow approximately 20–30 minutes into focused work. Thus, schedule deep-work sessions lasting at least 90 minutes, allowing sufficient time to achieve and sustain Flow.

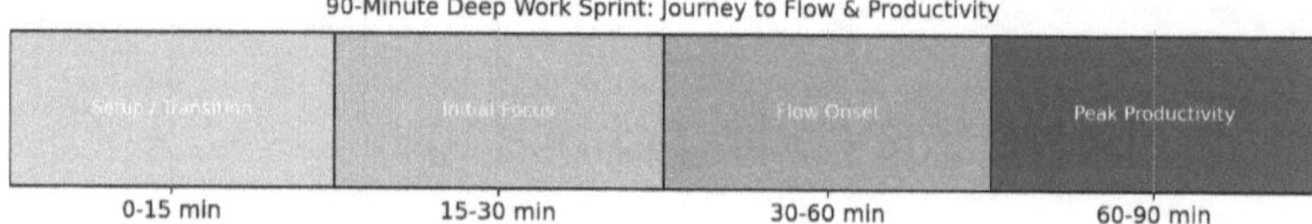

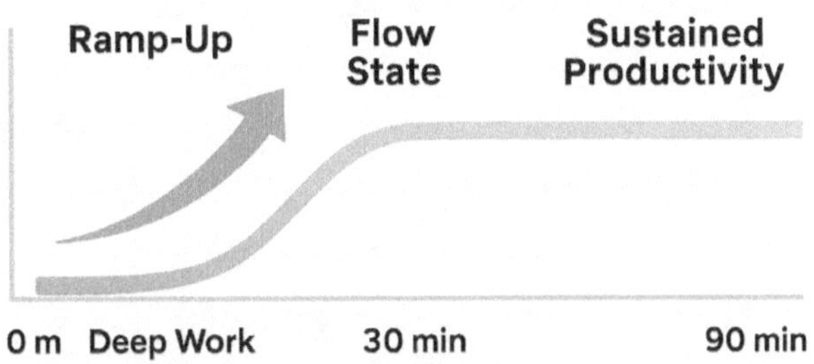

4. Develop Consistent Flow Rituals

Condition your brain with rituals signaling it's time for deep focus:

- Use consistent background music (instrumental, ambient).

- Perform brief activities like stretching or breathing exercises beforehand.

- Work from the same location each time you engage in deep work.

Rituals train your brain to rapidly enter Flow when desired.

Making Flow Your Default State

Before mastering flow:

- Difficulty maintaining deep concentration.

- Frequent procrastination or resistance to tasks.

- Limited productivity despite long hours.

After mastering flow:

★ Consistent access to deep, effortless concentration.

★ Increased enjoyment and productivity in work tasks.

★ Higher-quality results achieved in less time.

Chapter Summary

Flow is the peak state of effortless focus and productivity.

Achieve Flow by balancing challenge and skill, setting clear goals, and removing distractions.

Consistent rituals and deep-work scheduling enable frequent and reliable entry into Flow.

Next Chapter: The Distraction Trap—Why Your Brain Craves Interruptions (and How to Stop It)

Now that you can consistently enter Flow, it's critical to address external distractions that threaten this state. In **Chapter 7: The Distraction Trap**, you'll explore the true costs of interruptions and learn practical ways to defend your deep focus from constant digital interference.

References & Sources

1.	*Flow: The Psychology of Optimal Experience –
Mihaly Csikszentmihalyi -
https://www.harpercollins.com/products/flow-mihaly-csi
kszentmihalyi*

2.	*Harvard Business Review: How to Enter Flow
State on Demand -
https://hbr.org/2021/09/how-to-enter-flow-state-on-dem
and*

3.	*University of Chicago: Understanding the Flow
Experience -
https://news.uchicago.edu/explainer/what-flow*

Chapter 7

The Distraction Trap

How Interruptions Quietly Sabotage Your Productivity

You sit down, fully prepared to focus on your most important task. Minutes later, you instinctively reach for your phone, responding to a notification, checking social media, or quickly scanning your emails.

What just happened?

You didn't lack determination or discipline. Instead, you fell into the **Distraction Trap**—a subtle cycle perpetuated by your brain's craving for novelty and instant gratification.

Each notification or message triggers a dopamine hit, rewarding your brain for distraction. Over time, this cycle conditions your mind to seek interruptions, making sustained focus increasingly difficult.

This chapter reveals why distractions are so compelling, the hidden costs they impose, and proven methods to free yourself from this cycle.

The True Cost of Distractions

Most assume distractions cost only a few minutes of their day. The truth is far more severe:

• **23-Minute Refocus Penalty:** Each interruption requires approximately 23 minutes to fully regain deep focus. Five daily interruptions can cost nearly two productive hours each day—more than a full month per year.

• **Mental Energy Drain:** Frequent task-switching quickly exhausts cognitive resources, reducing overall productivity and increasing stress.

$$Total\ Time\ Lost = (Interruptions\ per\ Day) \times (23\ Minutes)$$

Let's do the math:

→ If you check your phone five times a day, that's nearly two hours of lost deep work—every single day.

➔   Over the course of a year, that adds up to over a full month of wasted productivity.

➔   This means that simply eliminating distractions could give you the equivalent of an extra month of focused work every year.

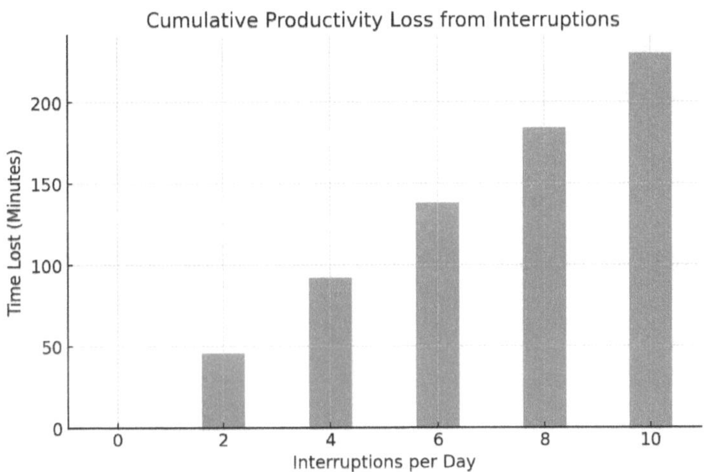

And it's not just about time—it's about **mental energy.**

Each time you switch tasks, your brain experiences a **cognitive switching penalty.** Instead of smoothly transitioning, it has to **reset, refocus, and rebuild momentum.**

If you allow **constant distractions**, you'll never reach a state of deep, uninterrupted focus—and your most meaningful work will suffer.

The Neuroscience Behind Your Craving for Distraction

Why is it so difficult to resist notifications or social media?

Each distraction triggers a dopamine release, reinforcing your brain's urge to seek out novelty and instant rewards:

Trigger (notification) → Action (check device) → Reward (dopamine release)

Over time, your brain learns that distractions feel rewarding, creating a powerful habit loop that undermines your productivity.

Dopamine Loop: The Distraction Cycle

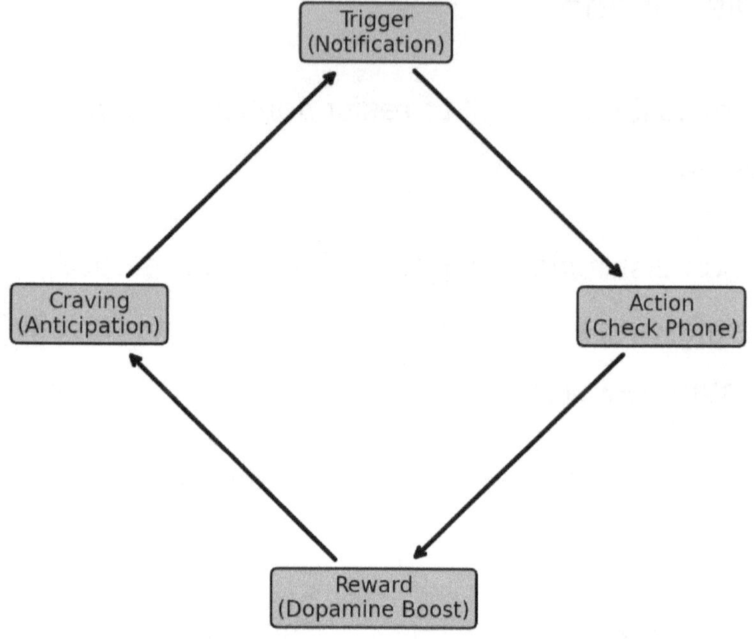

How to Break Free from the Distraction Trap

Escaping distractions requires more than willpower; it demands intentional restructuring of your environment and routines:

1. Implement the "10-Minute Rule"

Train your brain to delay gratification:

- When you feel the urge to check your phone, wait 10 minutes.

- Often, the craving will pass, gradually weakening the distraction habit.

2. Eliminate Non-Essential Notifications

Notifications constantly trigger dopamine-driven interruptions:

- Turn off alerts for social media, emails, and non-essential apps.

- Schedule specific times during the day for handling messages.

3. Designate "No-Distraction" Zones

Establish periods each day dedicated exclusively to deep work:

- Keep your phone in another room or on airplane mode.

- Communicate clearly to colleagues or family members about your protected time for uninterrupted work.

The Distraction-Free Productivity Equation

Reducing distractions has exponential impacts on productivity:

$$Productivity = \frac{(Total\,Work\,Hours \times Focus\,Intensity)}{(Interruptions + Switching\,Penalties)}$$

Fewer interruptions and less task-switching directly enhance your focus, making each hour spent working significantly more productive.

Conquering the Distraction Trap

Before addressing distractions:

- Frequent, impulsive device checks.

- Persistent task-switching and low productivity.

- Mental fatigue and stress from constant interruptions.

After eliminating distractions:

- ★ Longer periods of deep, uninterrupted work.

- ★ Improved productivity with reduced effort.

- ★ Greater satisfaction and reduced mental exhaustion.

Chapter Summary

Distractions incur substantial hidden costs, greatly diminishing your productivity and mental energy.

Dopamine-driven cycles reinforce your brain's addiction to frequent interruptions.

Strategic environmental adjustments and intentional habits break distraction cycles, enabling sustained deep focus.

Next Chapter: The Mental Reset—How to Recharge for Maximum Focus

Having learned how to identify and overcome distractions, the next step involves deliberately restoring mental energy for sustained productivity. In **Chapter 8: The Mental Reset**, you'll discover how intentional cognitive recovery throughout the day can dramatically boost your long-term ability to focus.

References & Sources

1.	*Worker Interrupted: The Cost of Task Switching – UC Irvine Study -* *https://www.ics.uci.edu/~gmark/chi08-mark.pdf*

2.	*Why the Modern World is Bad for Your Brain – The Guardian -* *https://www.theguardian.com/science/2015/jan/18/why-the-modern-world-is-bad-for-your-brain*

3.	*The Dopamine-Seeking Reward Loop – Psychology Today -* *https://www.psychologytoday.com/us/blog/the-dolphin-divide/201407/the-dopamine-seeking-reward-loop*

Chapter 8

The Mental Reset - How to Recharge for Maximum Focus

How Strategic Breaks Enhance Focus and Productivity

After hours of continuous work, you find yourself staring blankly at the screen, unable to concentrate. Despite your determination, your mind feels sluggish, and progress stalls.

This scenario highlights a critical truth: sustained productivity isn't solely about prolonged effort—it requires intentional mental resets.

In this chapter, you'll discover:

- The science behind mental fatigue and recovery.

- Effective strategies for incorporating restorative breaks.

- How to structure your day to maintain peak cognitive performance.

Understanding Mental Fatigue and Recovery

Your brain, like a muscle, tires after extended periods of exertion. Continuous cognitive activity depletes resources, leading to diminished focus, creativity, and decision-making abilities. Without adequate recovery, this fatigue accumulates, resulting in burnout and decreased productivity.

Research indicates that the brain operates optimally in cycles, typically engaging in focused work for about 90 minutes before requiring rest. Aligning your work habits with these natural rhythms enhances efficiency and well-being.

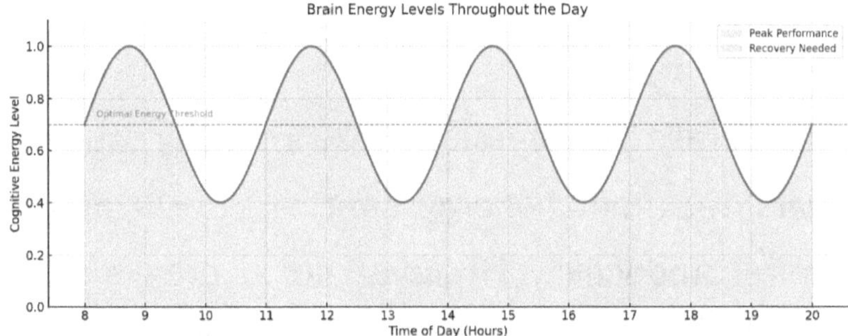

Here is the diagram illustrating the brain's cognitive energy levels across the day:

- The **blue zones** represent periods of **peak performance**, ideal for deep work.

- The **green zones** indicate times when **recovery is needed**, aligning with natural ultradian rhythms.

- The **dashed line** marks the optimal energy threshold—below this, fatigue may impact focus and productivity.

The Power of Strategic Breaks

Incorporating deliberate breaks into your routine revitalizes mental energy, sharpens focus, and boosts overall productivity. However, not all breaks are equally effective. The key lies in engaging in activities that promote genuine recovery.

Effective Mental Reset Techniques

1. **Physical Movement**

o Engage in light exercise, such as stretching or a brief walk, to increase blood flow and oxygenate the brain.

2. **Mindfulness and Meditation**

o Practice deep-breathing exercises or short meditation sessions to reduce stress and clear the mind.

3. **Nature Exposure**

○   Spend time outdoors or view scenes of nature to enhance mood and cognitive function.

4.   **Power Naps**

○   A brief nap of 10–20 minutes can significantly improve alertness and performance.

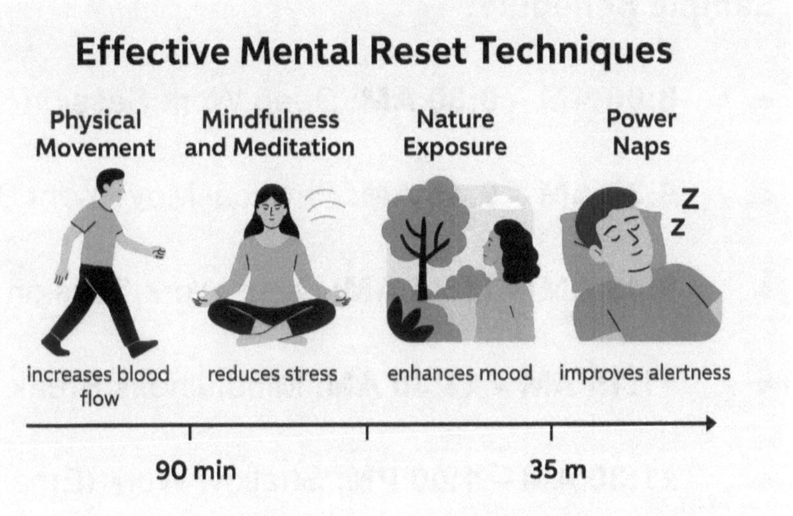

Structuring Your Day for Optimal Performance

To maximize productivity and maintain mental clarity, structure your workday to include regular intervals of focused work and restorative breaks.

Sample Schedule:

- **8:00 AM – 9:30 AM:** Deep Work Session

- **9:30 AM – 9:45 AM:** Physical Movement Break

- **9:45 AM – 11:15 AM:** Deep Work Session

- **11:15 AM – 11:30 AM:** Mindfulness Break

- **11:30 AM – 1:00 PM:** Shallow Work (Emails, Meetings)

- **1:00 PM – 2:00 PM:** Lunch and Relaxation

- **2:00 PM – 3:30 PM:** Deep Work Session

- **3:30 PM – 3:45 PM:** Nature Exposure Break

- **3:45 PM – 5:00 PM:** Shallow Work and Planning

This approach ensures that high-energy periods are dedicated to demanding tasks, while strategic breaks prevent burnout and sustain performance.

DAILY PLANNER

8:00 AM – 9:30 AM
Deep Work Session

9:30 AM – 9:45 AM
Physical Movement Break

9:45 – 11:15 AM
Deep Work Session

11:15 AM – 11:30 AM
Mindfulness Break

11:30 AM – 1:00 PM
Shallow Work
(Emails, Meetings)

1:00 PM – 2:00 PM
Lunch and Relaxation

2:00 PM – 3:30 PM
Deep Work Session

3:45 PM – 3:45 PM   **Shallow Work**
Nature Exposure   and Planning

The Mental Reset Formula: Designing a Brain-Friendly Routine

The secret to peak focus isn't just working smarter—it's recovering smarter.

$$Sustained\ Focus\ =\ \frac{Quality\ Rest + Strategic\ Breaks}{Cognitive\ Load + Mental\ Exhaustion}$$

By balancing deep work with intentional recovery, you extend your peak performance hours and reduce burnout.

Transforming Productivity Through Mental Resets

Before implementing strategic breaks:

• Prolonged periods of work leading to mental fatigue.

• Decreased concentration and productivity as the day progresses.

• Higher susceptibility to burnout and stress.

After incorporating mental resets:

★ Enhanced focus and sustained cognitive performance.

★ Improved mood and reduced stress levels.

★ Greater overall productivity and job satisfaction.

Chapter Summary

Mental fatigue impairs productivity; intentional breaks are essential for recovery.

Engaging in specific restorative activities during breaks enhances cognitive function.

Aligning work periods with natural energy cycles optimizes performance and well-being.

Next Chapter: The Focus Master's Advantage—How to Stay Ahead in an AI-Driven World

With a solid understanding of managing mental energy through strategic breaks, it's time to explore the evolving landscape of work. In **Chapter 9: The Focus Master's Advantage**, you'll examine how emerging technologies and changing work environments impact attention and productivity, and how to adapt effectively.

References & Sources

1.   *Worker Interrupted: The Cost of Task Switching – UC Irvine Study*

https://www.ics.uci.edu/~gmark/chi08-mark.pdf

2.   *Why the Modern World is Bad for Your Brain – The Guardian*

https://www.theguardian.com/science/2015/jan/18/why-the-modern-world-is-bad-for-your-brain

3.   *The Dopamine-Seeking Reward Loop – Psychology Today*

https://www.psychologytoday.com/us/blog/the-dolphin-divide/201407/the-dopamine-seeking-reward-loop

Chapter 9

The Focus Master's Advantage - Staying Ahead in an AI-Driven World

The Future Belongs to Those Who Can Focus

It's the year 2035.

You step into a café, open your laptop, and begin working. Around you, people jump between notifications, emails, and social media—barely scratching the surface of their tasks.

Meanwhile, you enter deep focus effortlessly, producing more valuable work in an hour than others do all day.

This scenario isn't far-fetched—it's the rapidly emerging reality of work.

As artificial intelligence continues to automate routine tasks, the most valuable skill in the workplace shifts from efficiency and speed to deep, strategic thinking that AI can't replicate.

This chapter explores why mastering deep focus is your greatest competitive advantage in an AI-driven economy, and provides practical ways to leverage this advantage effectively.

Why AI Won't Replace Deep Work

Artificial intelligence can rapidly analyze data, generate content, and even write code. But AI has clear limitations that skilled humans can exploit:

- **Original Creativity and Innovation:** AI excels at synthesizing existing ideas, but cannot authentically originate new ones.

- **Complex Problem-Solving and Strategic Thinking:** AI can process information but lacks human intuition, ethics, and long-term vision.

- **Deep Human Connection:** Empathy, leadership, and nuanced communication remain uniquely human strengths.

Those who can combine deep focus with these human skills will thrive in the AI era.

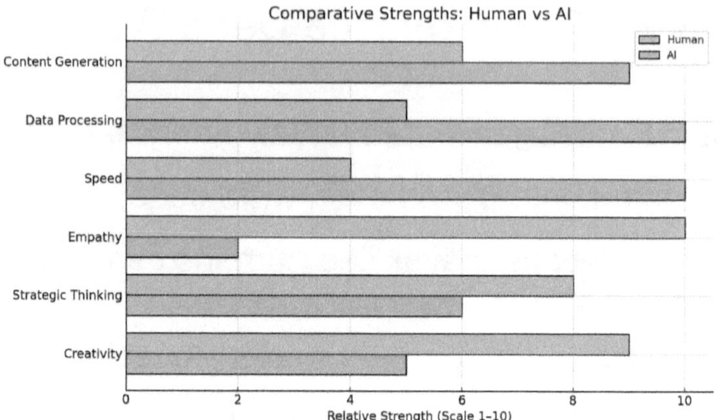

Comparative Strengths: Human vs AI
Human
AI
Content Generation
Data Processing
Speed
Empathy
Strategic Thinking
Creativity
0
2
4
6
8
10
Relative Strength (Scale 1–10)

How to Develop Your Competitive Advantage in an AI-Driven World

Mastering deep work positions you in the top tier of professionals. Here's how to harness this skill to remain competitive:

1. Structure Your Life Around Deep Work

The future elite won't necessarily work more—they'll work more deeply:

- Ruthlessly eliminate shallow tasks and distractions.

- Schedule protected deep work blocks consistently.

- Prioritize tasks requiring strategic thinking and creativity.

2. Cultivate Deep, Original Thinking

Your greatest advantage is your ability to think in ways that AI cannot:

•   Engage regularly in deep reflection, journaling, and brainstorming.

•   Consume fewer but higher-quality sources of information.

•   Shift from passive content consumption to active content creation.

3. Use AI to Complement Your Strengths

Instead of competing against AI, leverage it as a productivity enhancer:

•   Delegate repetitive tasks to AI (e.g., data sorting, scheduling, research summaries).

•   Focus your time on tasks requiring uniquely human insight and creativity.

The Focus Master's Advantage Equation

Your success in an AI-driven future will depend heavily on how effectively you focus:

$$Future\ Success\ =\ \frac{(Deep\ Focus \times Human\ Creativity)}{(Distractions + AI\ Competition)}$$

Reducing distractions and strategically leveraging AI maximizes your unique human strengths, positioning you ahead of automation.

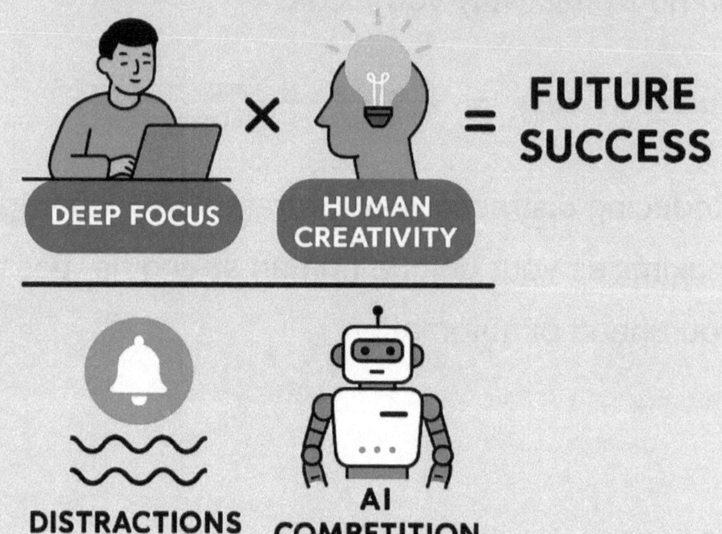

THE FOCUS MASTER'S ADVANTAGE EQUATION
DEEP FOCUS
HUMAN CREATIVITY
FUTURE SUCCESS
DISTRACTIONS
AI COMPETITION

Preparing for the AI Future

Before mastering deep focus:

- Constantly distracted and reactive.

- Overwhelmed by information overload and digital clutter.

- Vulnerable to being replaced or outperformed by automation.

After mastering deep focus:

★ Consistent high-quality, innovative output.

★ Leveraging AI to enhance productivity rather than competing against it.

★ Positioned as an irreplaceable leader and creative thinker.

Chapter Summary

The rise of AI increases demand for uniquely human skills like creativity, strategy, and empathy.

Deep focus differentiates you, enabling original thought and high-value work.

Combining deep work with AI tools multiplies your competitive advantage.

Final Thoughts: Your Focus, Your Future

Having understood how deep work positions you advantageously in the AI era, you now possess the insights and tools to thrive in a rapidly evolving workplace. Next, you'll see clearly how cultivating this mastery over focus can reshape your professional future—and life—in the concluding chapter, "The Power of Focus in a Distracted World."

References & Sources

1.	*The Future of Jobs Report – World Economic Forum -*
https://www.weforum.org/reports/the-future-of-jobs-report-2023

2.	*Why Humans Are Still Better Than AI at Creativity – Harvard Business Review -*
https://hbr.org/2019/08/why-humans-are-still-better-than-ai-at-creativity

3.	*Human Skills in the AI Economy – Deloitte Insights -*
https://www2.deloitte.com/us/en/insights/focus/human-capital-trends/2020/beyond-reskilling-human-skills-ai-era.html

Conclusion

The Power of Focus in a Distracted World

Your Competitive Advantage in the Age of Distraction

Every morning, before you even leave your bed, your attention is under siege.

Notifications buzz. Emails accumulate. Social media feeds update. The relentless news cycle clamors for your attention. By the time you sit down to work, your mind is already overwhelmed, scattered, and unable to deeply engage with meaningful tasks.

This daily battle for attention isn't unique to you—it defines our era.

Yet, within this distracted world lies a powerful opportunity. Those who master their attention and consistently engage in deep, meaningful work hold a distinct advantage. They achieve significantly more with less effort.

You now have the tools to join them.

The New Divide: Distracted vs. Focused

In the modern workplace, success is increasingly determined not by working longer hours or multitasking but by mastering deep, focused attention.

Distracted Majority:

- Reactive to every notification and email.

- Task-switching frequently, diminishing productivity.

- Exhausted, overstimulated, and creatively depleted.

Focused Elite:

- Deliberate in controlling attention and environment.

- Consistently entering deep states of productivity.

- Achieving higher-quality output with fewer working hours.

The difference isn't talent or intelligence—it's disciplined attention management.

Your Deep Work Advantage Equation

You now understand how to unlock productivity through deep focus:

$$Deep\ Work\ Mastery = \frac{Total\ Work\ Hours \times Focus\ Intensity}{Distractions + Cognitive\ Switching\ Penalty}$$

By intentionally minimizing distractions and task-switching, you increase the intensity of your focus—producing exponentially better results in less time.

Your Next Steps: Turning Knowledge into Action

Understanding the power of deep focus is the first step. Transforming that knowledge into tangible results requires action. Start today by implementing these essential strategies:

1. Optimize Your Environment for Focus

- Remove distractions (notifications, unnecessary tabs, clutter).

- Create rituals that signal to your brain when it's time for deep work.

- Work in consistent, distraction-free spaces.

2. Rewire Your Brain for Deep Work

- Replace impulsive scrolling with intentional activities (reading, journaling, deep thinking).

- Regularly practice techniques that improve sustained concentration.

- Deliberately schedule deep-work sessions daily.

3. Embrace Original Thinking

- Prioritize tasks requiring creativity, problem-solving, and strategic thinking.

- Limit shallow tasks by automating, delegating, or batching.

- Leverage AI to handle repetitive tasks, freeing your attention for deep work.

Final Thoughts: Your Future Depends on Your Focus

In an increasingly distracted world, your ability to concentrate deeply becomes your greatest asset. Those who master deep work will not only rise above the distractions but also shape the future of innovation and creativity.

Your future is defined by how effectively you use your attention.

You now hold the blueprint—it's time to put it into action.

Choose focus.
Choose depth.
Shape your future.

Final Steps: Maintaining Your Deep Work Habit

Remember, deep work mastery is not a one-time achievement. It is a continuous practice that compounds over time:

- Regularly revisit the concepts in this book.

- Continually refine your work habits and environment.

- Measure your progress and adjust your strategies accordingly.

Your journey into deep work mastery is just beginning—and its rewards will only grow more substantial over time.

Thank You

A Personal Note from the Author

Thank you for reading *The Math of Focus, Creativity, and Deep Work*. I wrote this book to help people like you reclaim their attention, unlock their mental potential, and do the work that truly matters.

If you've made it this far, I hope you've found not only practical strategies but also inspiration to take ownership of your time, energy, and focus. The ability to work deeply and think clearly is no longer just a productivity skill—it's a life advantage.

Remember: this isn't the end of your journey. It's the beginning of a new way of working, thinking, and living.

I'd Love to Hear From You

If this book helped you, inspired you, or changed the way you think about your work—even in a small way—I'd truly appreciate your support in one of the following ways:

Leave a Review

Your honest review helps other readers discover this book and join the movement toward deeper, more meaningful work. Whether it's a sentence or a full reflection, I read every one—and your words matter.

➤ Please consider leaving a review on your preferred platform (Amazon, Goodreads, etc.).

Thank you again for investing your time and trust in this book.

Now go do the work that matters—boldly, creatively, and with deep focus.

With gratitude,

Elara Juan Morris